For
Alexandra

First U.S. edition 2020
First published by Berbay Publishing (Australia) 2018

Library of Congress Catalog Card Number 2020906232
ISBN 978-1-5362-0784-2

22 23 24 25 APS 10 9 8 7 6 5 4 3

Printed in Humen, Dongguan, China

This book was typeset in Passport.
The illustrations were done in watercolor and, except for
the stick insect, butterfly, caterpillar, and chrysalis, were
adapted from *Animals: 1,419 Copyright-Free Illustrations of
Mammals, Birds, Fish, Insects, Etc.* (New York: Dover, 1979).

Candlewick Press
99 Dover Street
Somerville, Massachusetts 02144

visit us at www.candlewick.com

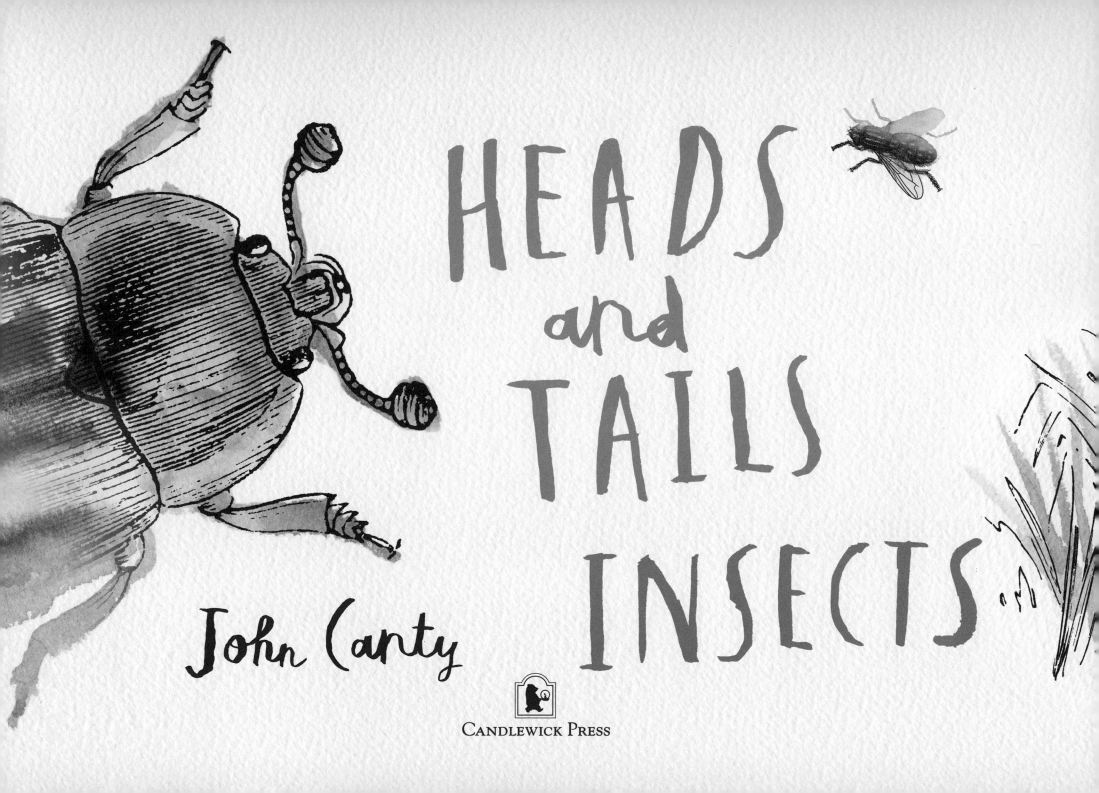

HEADS and TAILS INSECTS

John Canty

CANDLEWICK PRESS

I live in a hive.

I make honey.

I can sting you.

I AM A . . .

BEE.

I have a spotted
red body.

I have a domed shell
that protects my wings.

I am called a lady
even if I am a male.

I AM A ...

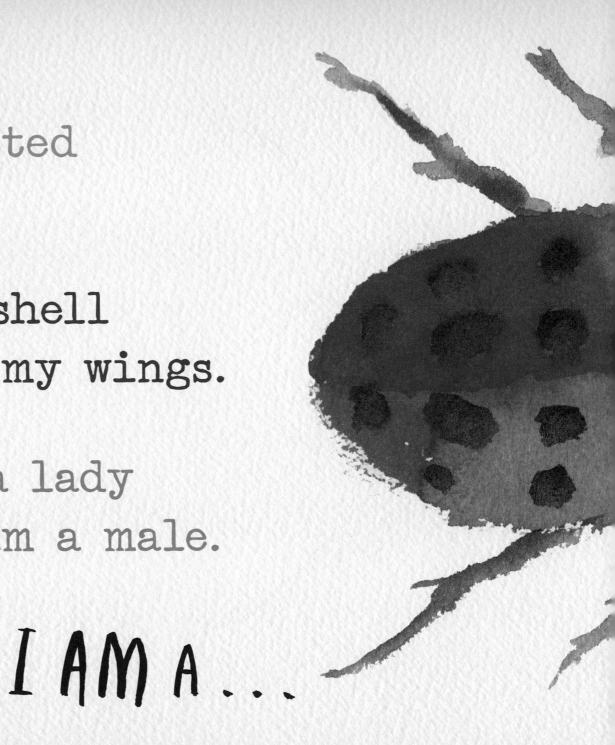

LADYBUG.

I have large hind legs.

I can hop great distances.

I make music by rubbing my hind leg against my wing.

I AM A . . .

GRASSHOPPER.

I visit you
on warm nights.

I buzz in your ear
and keep you awake.

I can bite you
and suck your blood.

I AM A . . .

MOSQUITO.

I am as agile as a cat.

I am a master
of camouflage.

I look like
I am praying.

I AM A . . .

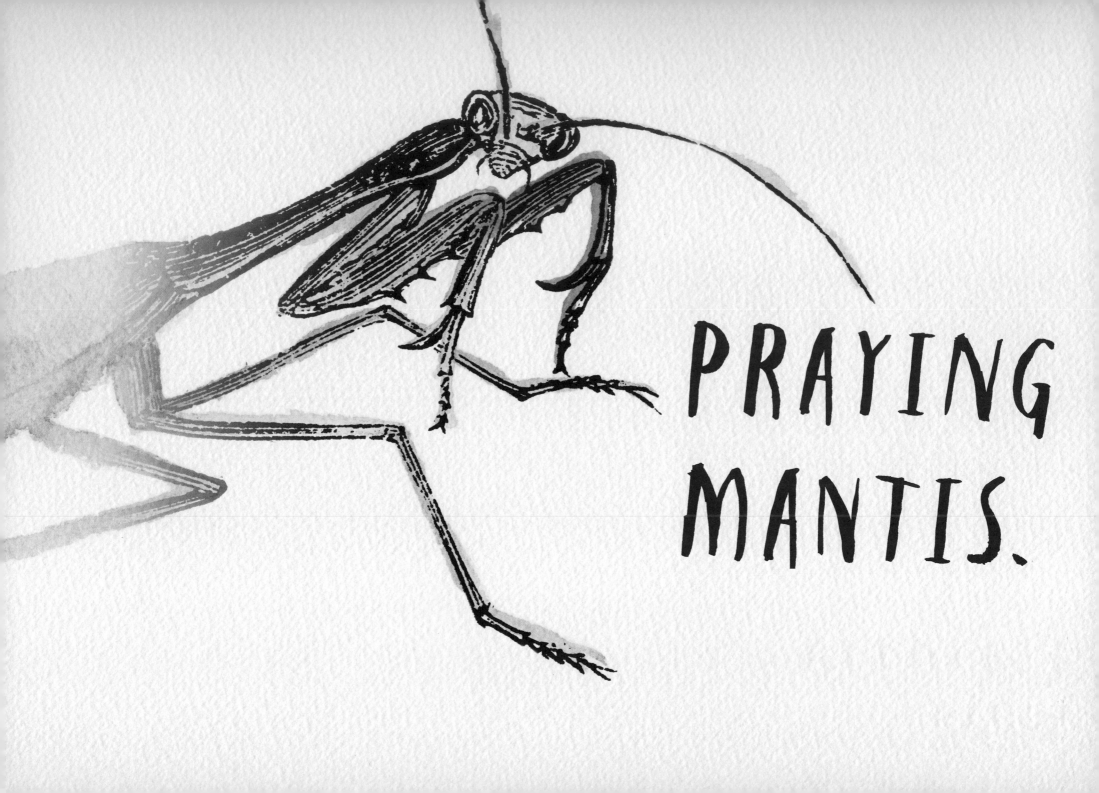

PRAYING MANTIS.

I crawl in a wavelike motion.

I have a soft body.

I build a cocoon.

CATERPILLAR.

I was once
a caterpillar.

Now I have beautiful
colored wings.

I flutter from
flower to flower.

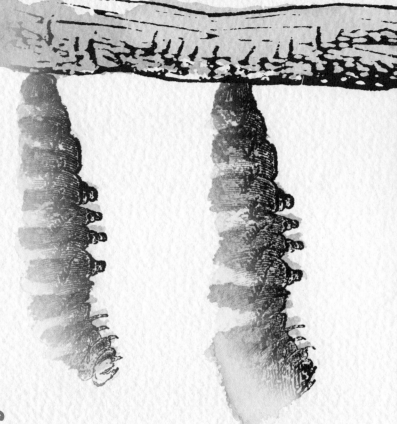

I AM...

A...

BUTTERFLY.

I have four wings.

I can fly up and down
and from side to side.

I look scary,
but I am harmless.

I AM A . . .

DRAGONFLY.

I buzz around your face
and food and annoy you.

I have sticky feet and
can walk upside down.

If I get stuck in a web,
a spider will eat me.

I AM A . . .

FLY.

I come in many
different colors.

I belong to the largest
order of insects.

I eat leaves, seeds,
and fruit.

I AM A . . .

BEETLE.

I have a long,
   thin body.

I look like
   a stick.

   I am very good
   at hiding.

   I AM A . . .

STICK INSECT.

I live with millions
of family and friends.

We **march** together
in long lines.

I can carry many
times my own weight.

I AM AN...

ANT.